TREASURE HUNT MAZES

by Roger Moreau

Treasure Castle Map

Start • End

King's Forest • Canyon of Rivers • The Great Castles • Castle Mountain

Sterling Publishing Co, Inc.

New York

10 9 8 7 6 5 4 3 2 1

Published by Sterling Publishing Company, Inc.

387 Park Avenue South, New York, N.Y. 10016

© 2001 by Roger Moreau

Distributed in Canada by Sterling Publishing

C/o Canadian Manda Group, One Atlantic Avenue, Suite 105

Toronto, Ontario, Canada M6K 3E7

Distributed in Great Britain and Europe by Chris Lloyd at Orca Book Services,

Stanley House, Fleets Lane, Poole BH15 3AJ, England

Distributed in Australia by Capricorn Link (Australia) Pty. Ltd.

P.O. Box 704, Windsor, NSW 2756 Australia

Sterling ISBN 0-8069-6633-5

Contents

A Note on the Suggested Use of This Book

As you work your way through the pages of this book, try not to mark them. It is suggested that you use tracing paper to mark on. This will enable you to take the journey over and over again and will give your friends a challenge to take the same journey that you took with all of the same challenges that you had to face.

Special Warning: When the way looks too difficult, avoid the temptation to start at the end and work your way backwards. This technique would be a violation of the rules and would result in having to return any treasures that you find.

Cover Maze: The dark tiles are trapdoors that are instant death. Stay on the light tiles. You can only move at right or left angles. Do not move at a diagonal. Try to reach the red carpet. Then find a clear path to the rope at the window to escape. Pick up as much treasure as you can.

Introduction

"My name is Baron Von Maze and I am the keeper of the castle. Many centuries ago I led a band of warriors across our borders to find and return treasures that had been stolen from our country by bandits and foreign enemies. The quest took years and cost many lives, but we prevailed and were able to return the stolen treasures to our homeland.

"A castle fortress was built to house and protect the treasures and I was appointed to the highest rank and honor that our country can bestow: the rank of Baron and the honor of 'Keeper of The Castle.'

"Our country was ruled for many years by a good and just king. When he died, there followed a reign of wicked kings and unjust rulers. I alone successfully protected the castle treasures from falling into their evil hands, by creating a variety of obstacles throughout the castle. Over time, there were many attempts to steal the treasures, but all failed. I also kept a journal that will give clués to the location of the castle and the treasures. I hid this journal before I passed away, with plans for it to come forth at that special time when my treasures shall be delivered up to a just and honorable person.

"That time is now! At last all of this wealth can be put to good use. It will be important for the *right* person to find the castle and its treasures. That person is *you*."

The Baron was very careful to safeguard the treasure because he knew that when he died, villains would still be alive that could use the wealth in an unjust way. He reasoned that the passing of time would cause the castle to become unimportant and blend in with all of the other castles in the land. The villains would die off and the treasure's whereabouts would become unknown. The treasure could then be available for the right person when that time came along.

Planning for these possibilities, Baron Von Maze kept a journal that carefully documented many things that would help the right person find his or her way to the castle. In the journal, he placed a very important map and wrote down many clues that could only be recognized through a good person's wisdom. To prevent this valuable journal from falling into the wrong hands, he hid it in the basement of the local town storage facility, tucked in among the many stacks of old papers and books.

The reasoning of the Baron proved to be true, and the castle eventually became one of the many abandoned relics of the land, with the treasure forgotten and intact.

A number of years ago, archaeologists came upon those old books in the storage facility and moved them to a storage room in the government library, where they now collect dust. They are sealed off from the public, awaiting the time when they can be looked over and cataloged. The journal is there. The first step on your journey to locate the castle and find the treasure is to get into that room and find Baron Von Maze's journal. To proceed without it would be folly.

The Journal

The Baron's journal is here. To find it, get to the ladder and climb it. Total the numbers in each row of books. Put each total on the journal at the end of the row. The journal with the highest number is the Baron's journal. Take the journal with you on your journey.

Start

The Map

Look carefully at this map from the journal and work the mazes by finding a clear path. This will give you some idea of what's ahead.

Treasure

Start

King's Forest   Canyon of Rivers

stle Map

End

The Great Castles   Castle Mountain

The King's Forest

Find a clear path through the forest and continue to the canyon of rivers.

Start
Exit
on the right

Canyon Path

Cross over the canyons on the logs until you reach the other side.

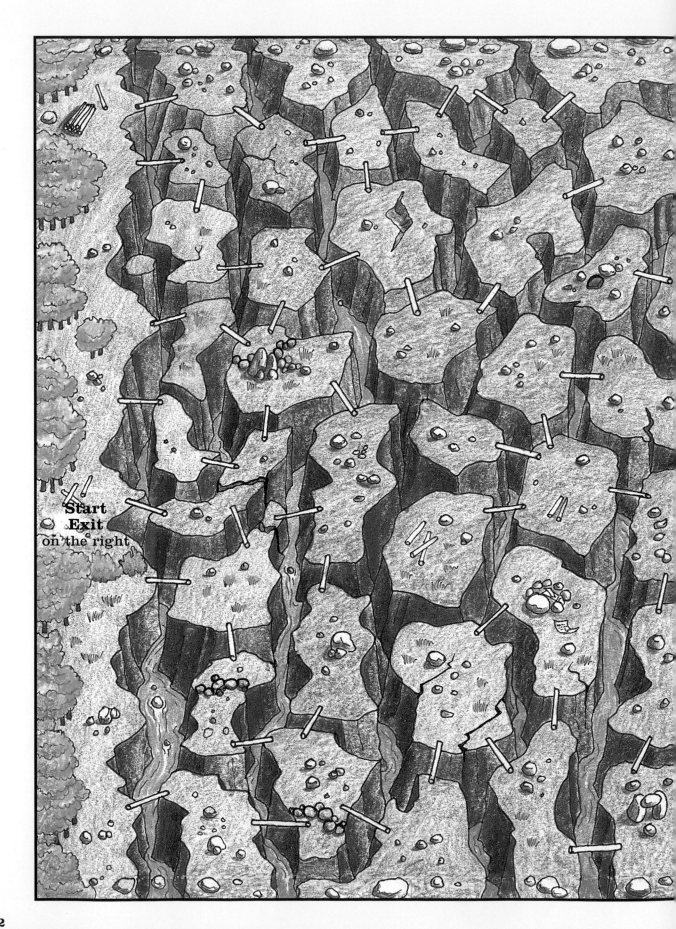

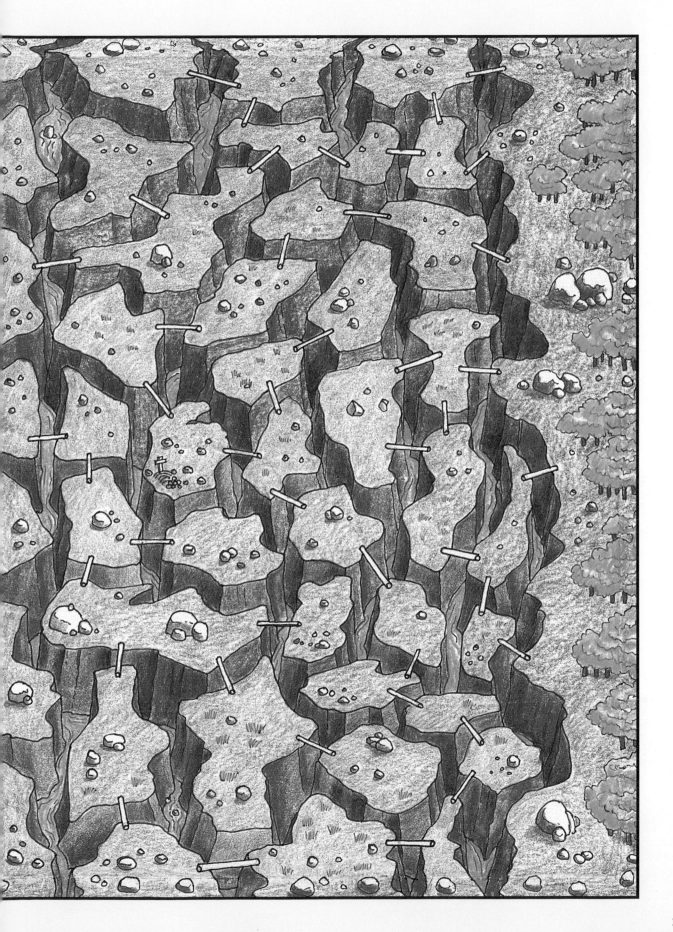

The Great Castles

On the hill are four of the old forgotten castles of long ago. One is the Baron's treasure castle. But which one? Only one path will get you to the base of the hill that the treasure castle is on.

Castle Mountain

Find a clear path to the top of Castle Mountain.

The Graveyard

The journal tells of a secret tunnel that bypasses the alligator-infested moat. This grave-yard has been plundered in an effort to find it. The journal says to find a clear path to the tomb at the top of the hill.

Enter

Start

The Secret Tunnel

Find a clear way to the castle drawbridge on the other side of the moat.

The Drawbridge

To drop the drawbridge, climb the connected protruding blocks and cut the ropes on both sides of the bridge that descend to the ground.

The Grating

To get through this grating, move your way up through the openings and crawl through the big opening near the top.

The Courtyard

Find a clear path through the castle courtyard and enter through one of the doors on the right.

Start
Exit
on the
right

The Banquet Room

Robbers, over the years, have ransacked everything in an effort to find the treasure. The Baron left it this way to discourage others. Find your way around the objects and move into the next room through one of the doors on the right.

The Weapons Room

As was done in the banquet room, move around the weapons and exit on the right.

Exit

The Room of Armor

Suits of armor lie as they fell when they were taken off after battle. Find a clear path to the door on the right.

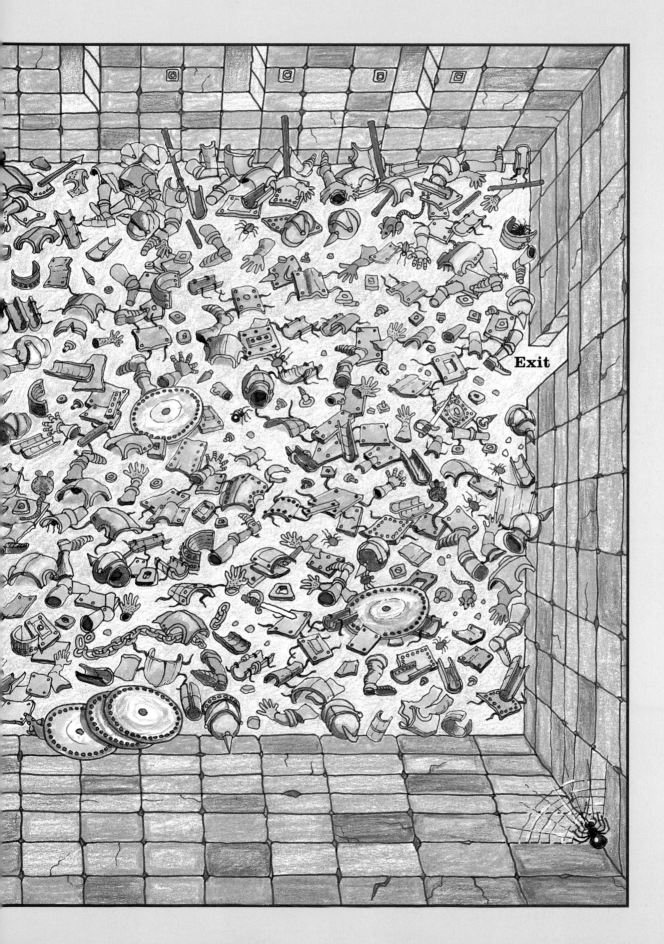

Exit

The Jail

Those who were caught seeking the treasure were placed in this jail. None escaped. Find your way to the doorway on the right.

Exit

The Tower

Climb the circular stairway. You can go up and down on the ladders to get to the door at the top.

You have done very well to have journeyed this far without getting lost or giving up. The journal has probably been a big help. There are many dangers still ahead. As you get closer to the treasures, the Baron set some dangers that only tips from the journal will get you through safely. So be careful. Follow those tips unfailingly and you will succeed.

As you enter the room at the top of the stairs, notice that some of the tiles are light and some are dark. *Danger!* Do not proceed until you have read the journal regarding this room.

Good Luck!

Trapdoors! Look Out!

This room was designed by the Baron to stop anyone who had gotten this far. The floor is a maze of trapdoors. From the journal, he has given to you an important clue to

Start

getting safely to the door on the right. Do not step on any dark tiles. You can only move straight or at right or left angles. You cannot move at a diagonal.

Getting Close

Can you feel the tension mount? Keys and locked doors: this is a sign that you are getting close. Find the key that will unlock the right door. Do not step on a dark trap door, or you are history.

Start
Exit
on the
right

The Mystery Key Room

This door has the king's crest on it. The problem is it's locked. Which is the right key? Here's another journal clue: Add the numbers *vertically* on each row and place the total at the top of each row. Add up the minus numbers on each key at the top. Subtract the total of the minus numbers from the total in each row. The number that matches on the hanging key is the right key.

The Treasure Room

Avoid the dark-square trapdoors and move to the red carpet. At last the treasure is yours. Exit out the window opening.

Canon Defenses

Your challenge now is to escape from the castle. The journal indicates that an addition to the castle was built in later years to help the right person escape. Make your way across this defense area of cannons to the new addition at the right.

Start

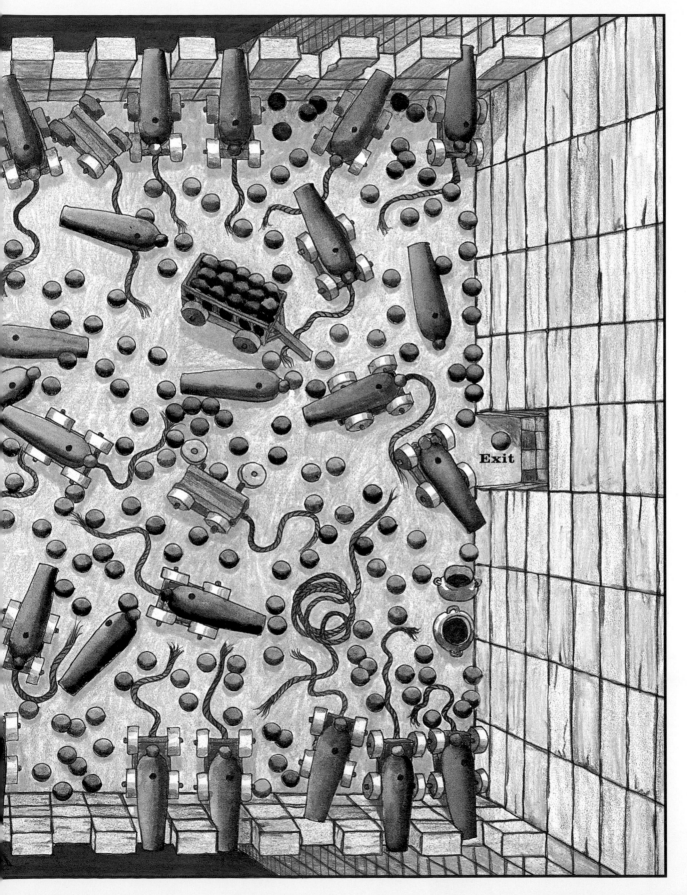

Exit

The Golden Idol

What? More treasure? This golden idol was a gift from an Egyptian king. This room was built especially for the idol and placed on the escape route for you. Dark trapdoors protect the idol, so be careful. Exit out any of the surrounding doors.

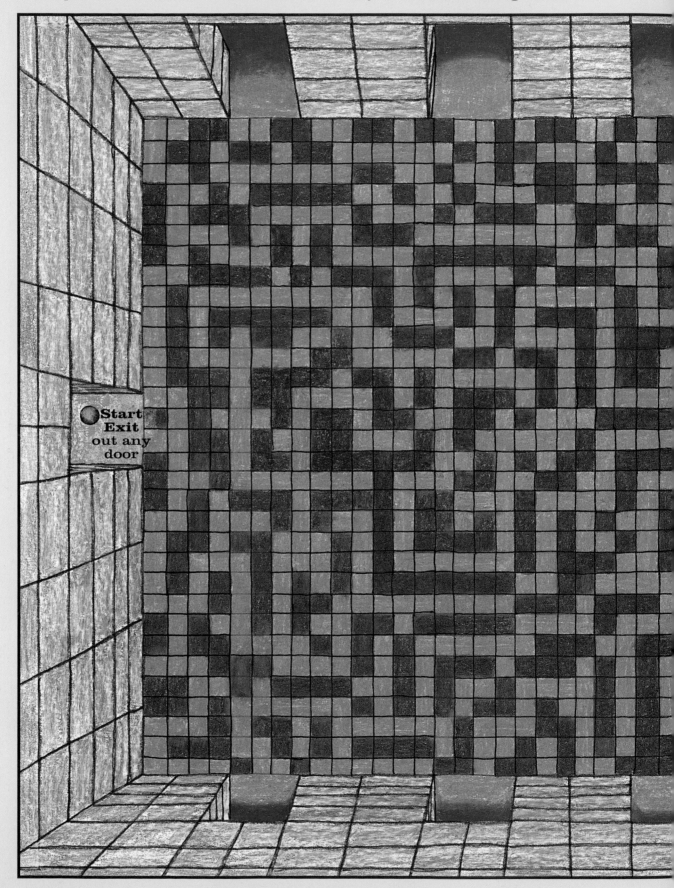

The Shaft

Find your way down the shaft by going up or down unbroken ladders.

Exit

Start through any door.

Look out!
When you touched the idol, conditions were set in motion that have caused stone blocks to fall. This was done in an effort to stop robbers and bandits from escaping with the treasures.

There is no way to stop the blocks from falling, so keep your eyes open and try not to get under any as you find your way out of the castle.

Oh, No! Rats!

Old castles are full of rats. This looks like the whole family. Avoid them and hurry to the door on the right.

Exit

The Collapsing Floor

This floor is broken up and collapsing. Hurry through to the door on the right.

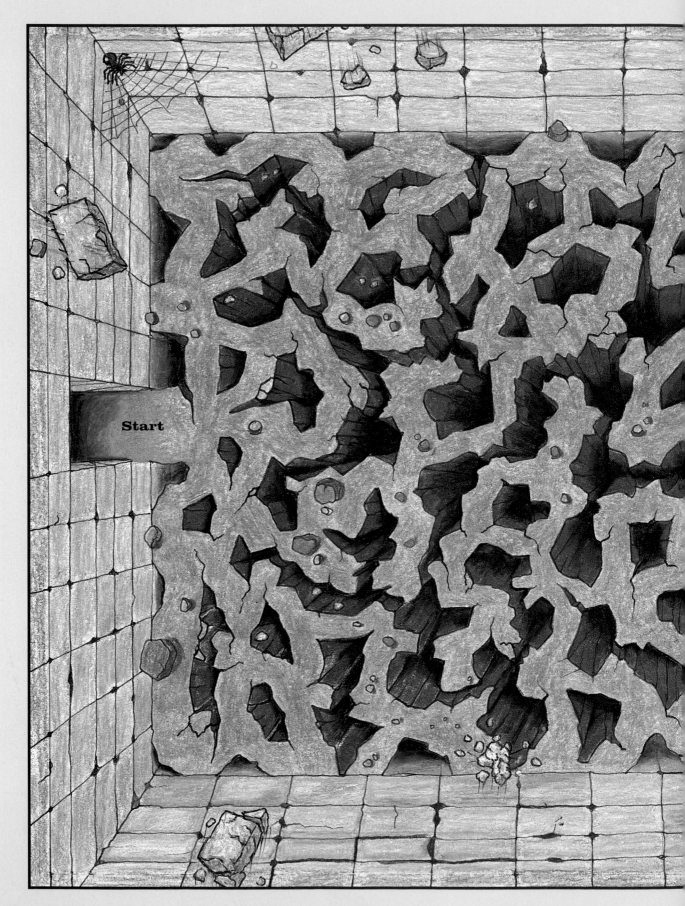

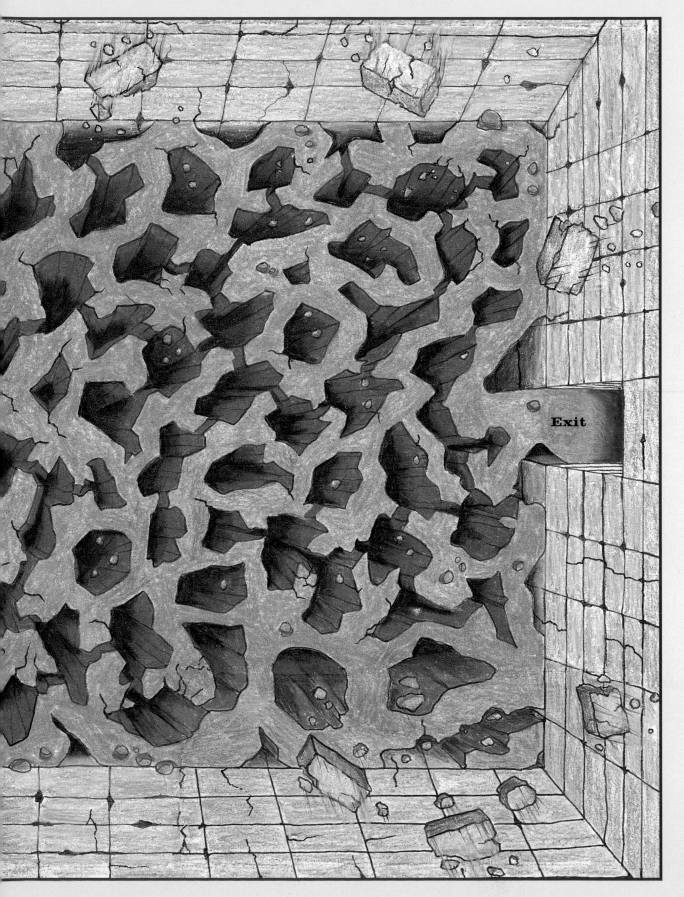

Exit

The Junk Room

It looks like the door at the top goes to the outside. But wait! The journal says to exit through the trapdoor. Find a clear path to it and do not go out the door.

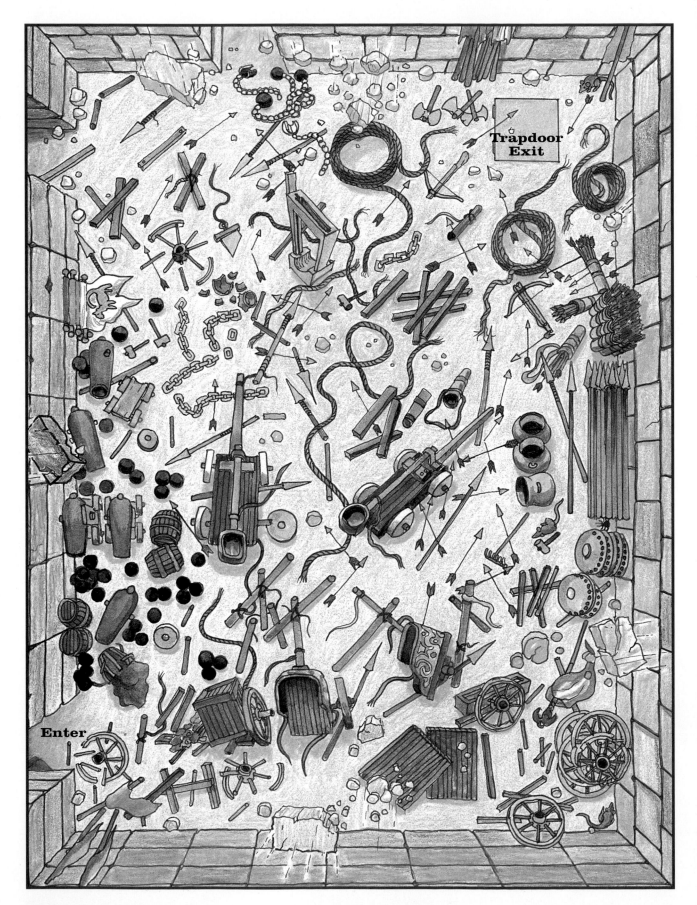

The Escape Tunnel

Find your way through the tunnel to the door on the far side of the moat.

Congratulations

Your wonderful adventure has ended with great success. You have found and brought back a great deal of Baron Von Maze's treasure. You deserve all of the wealth that you have risked your life to find. You will put it to good use. That is why the Baron trusted you to find it. But you were not able to carry out all of the treasures, so go back. Go back as many times as necessary to get all of the treasure, and take a good person you can trust with you.

If you have trouble along the way, check the solutions on the following pages. Do not refer to these solutions until *after* you complete your journey.

Cover Maze Solution/The Journal

Treasure Castle Map

Start

End

King's Forest   Canyon of Rivers   The Great Castles   Castle Mountain

The King's Forest

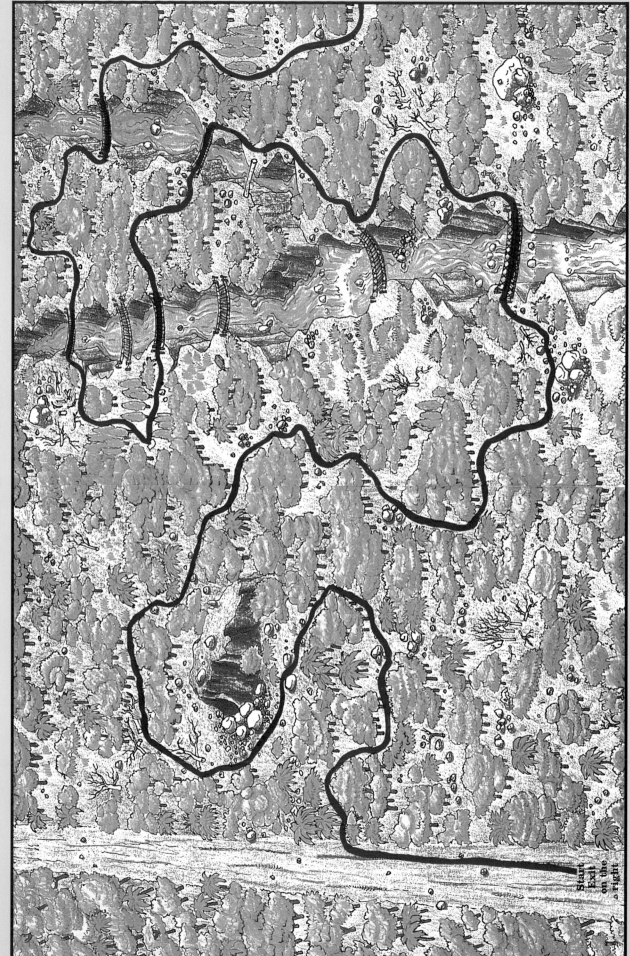

Start. Exit on the right.

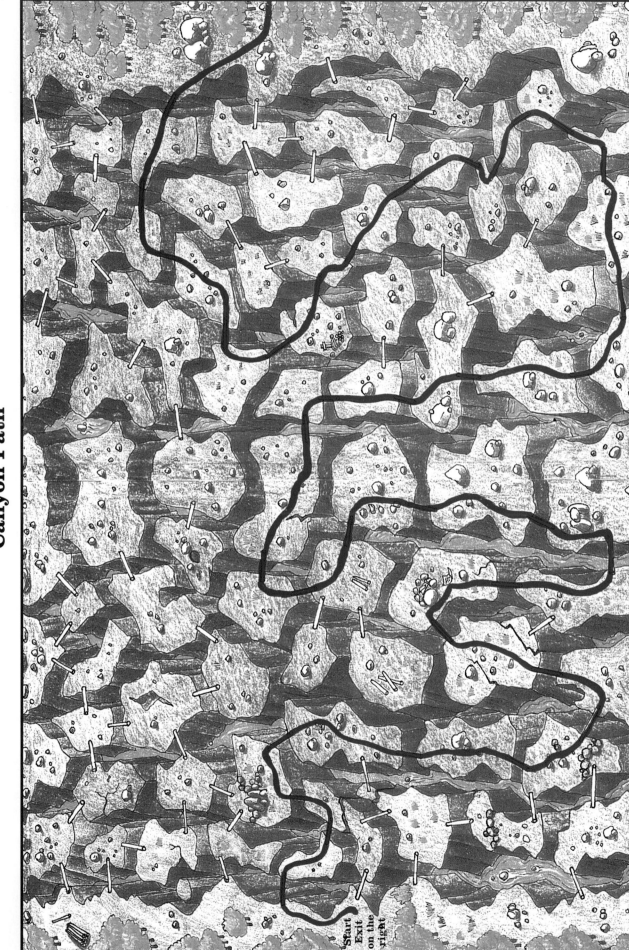

Start
Exit
on the
right

The Great Castles

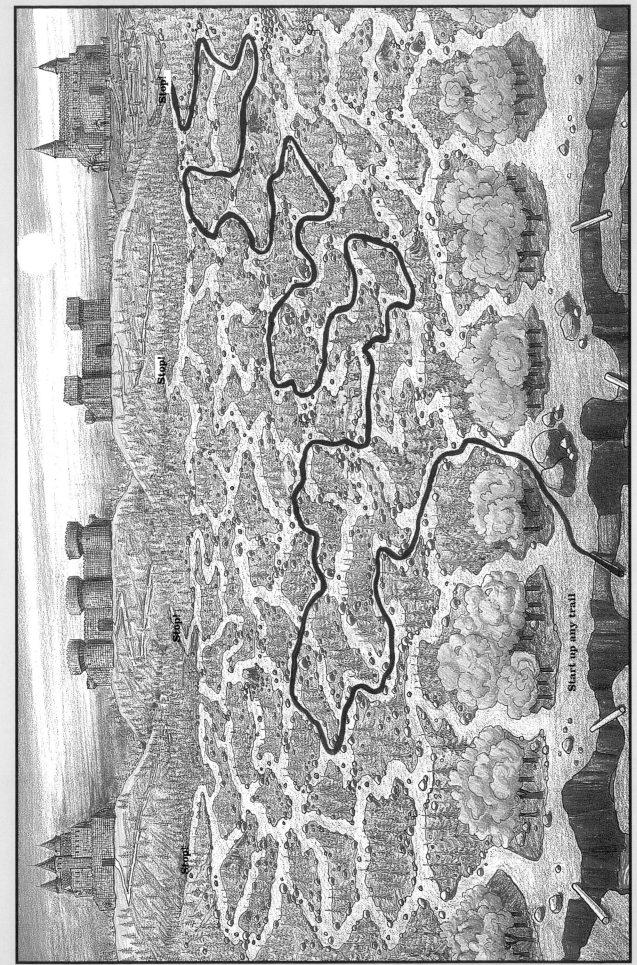

Castle Mountain

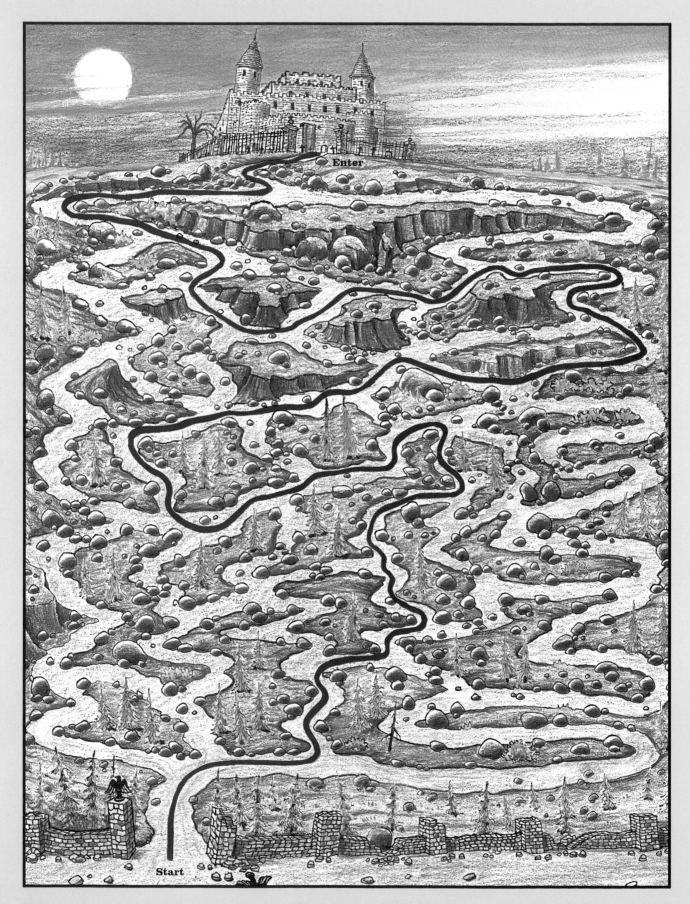

Enter

Start

The Graveyard

Enter

Start

The Secret Tunnel

The Drawbridge

Start

End

The Grating

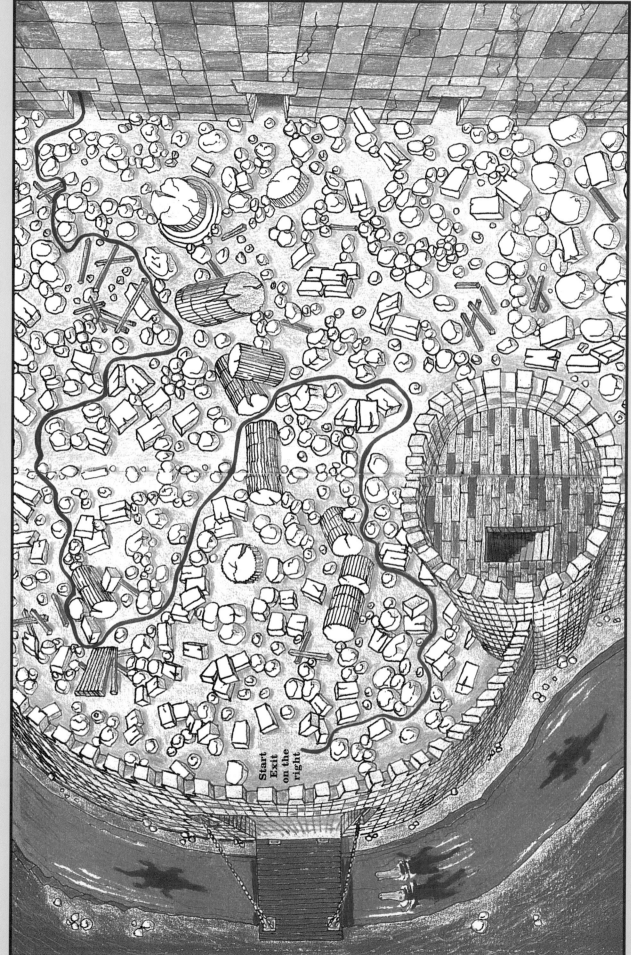

Start
Exit
on the
right

The Banquet Room

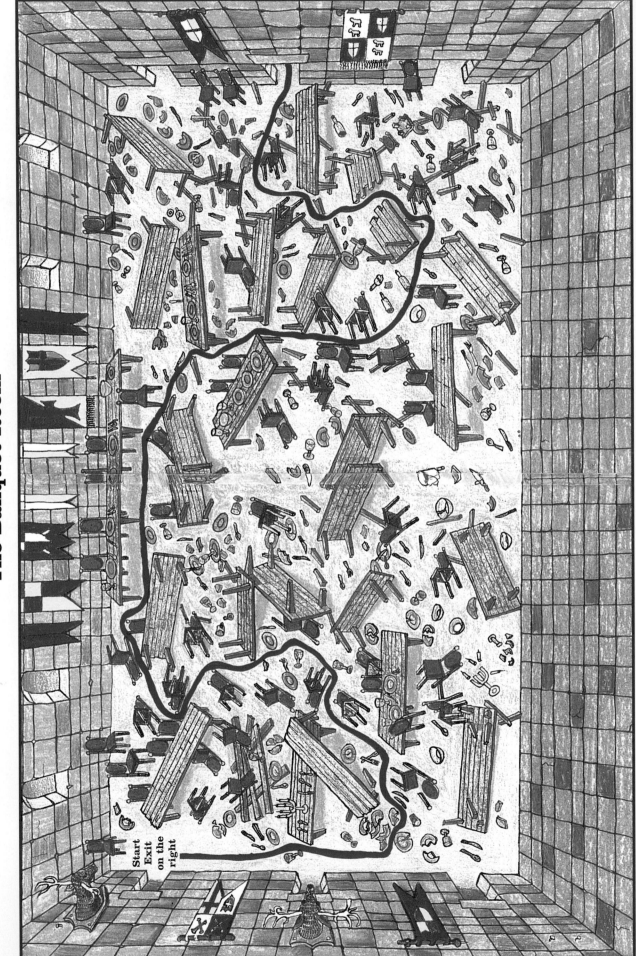

Start Exit on the right

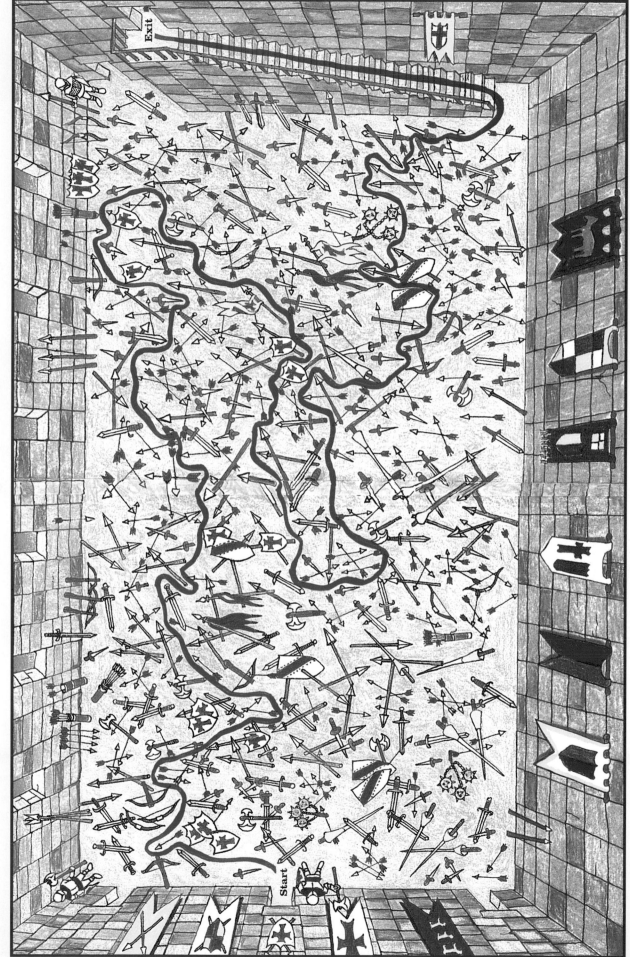

The Room of Armor

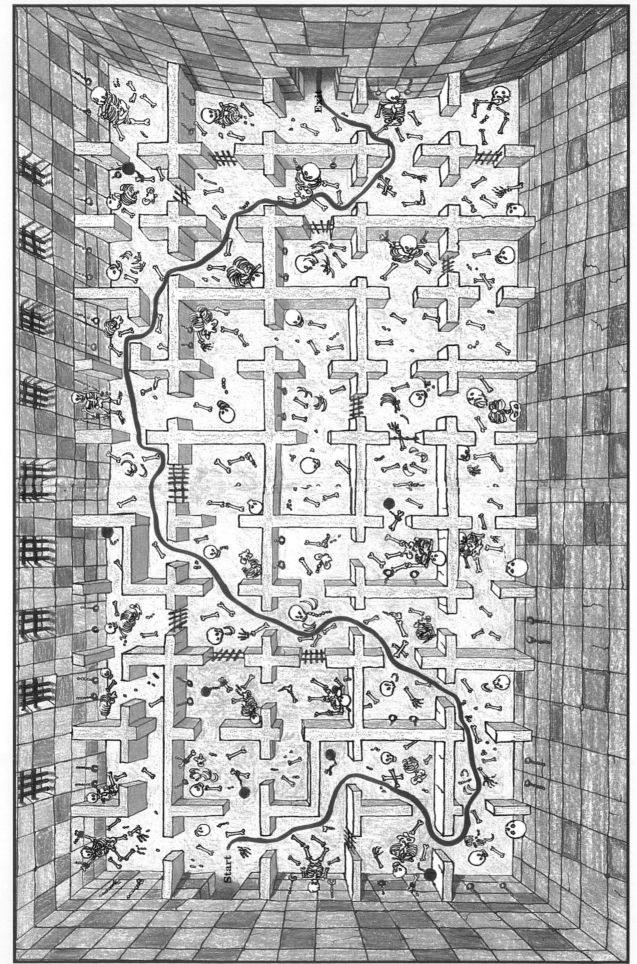

The Jail

Start

Exit

The Tower

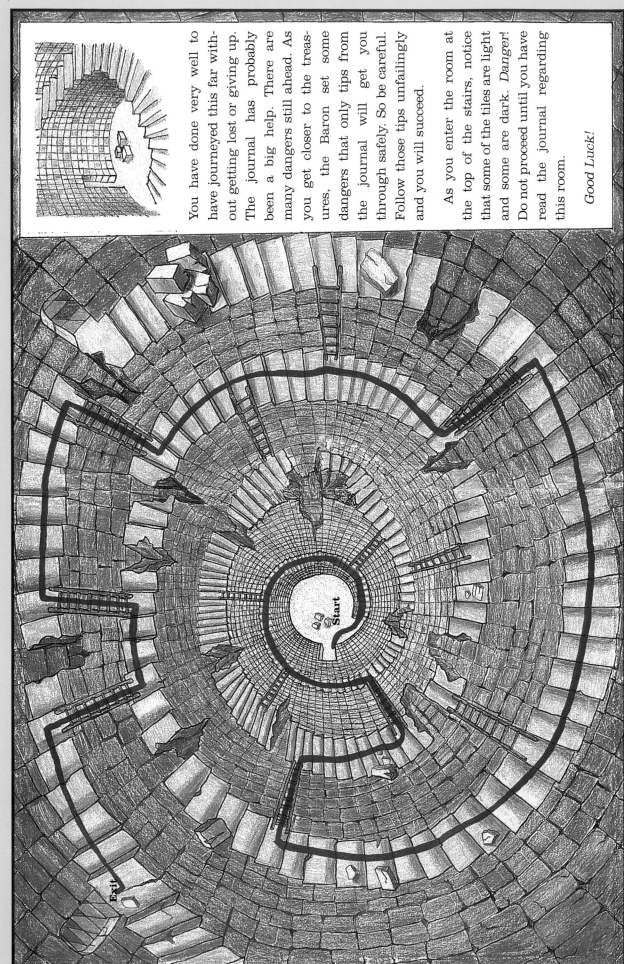

You have done very well to have journeyed this far without getting lost or giving up. The journal has probably been a big help. There are many dangers still ahead. As you get closer to the treasures, the Baron set some dangers that only tips from the journal will get you through safely. So be careful. Follow those tips unfailingly and you will succeed.

As you enter the room at the top of the stairs, notice that some of the tiles are light and some are dark. *Danger!* Do not proceed until you have read the journal regarding this room.

Good Luck!

Start

Exit

Trapdoors! Look Out!

Getting Close

Start
Exit
on the
right

The Mystery Key Room

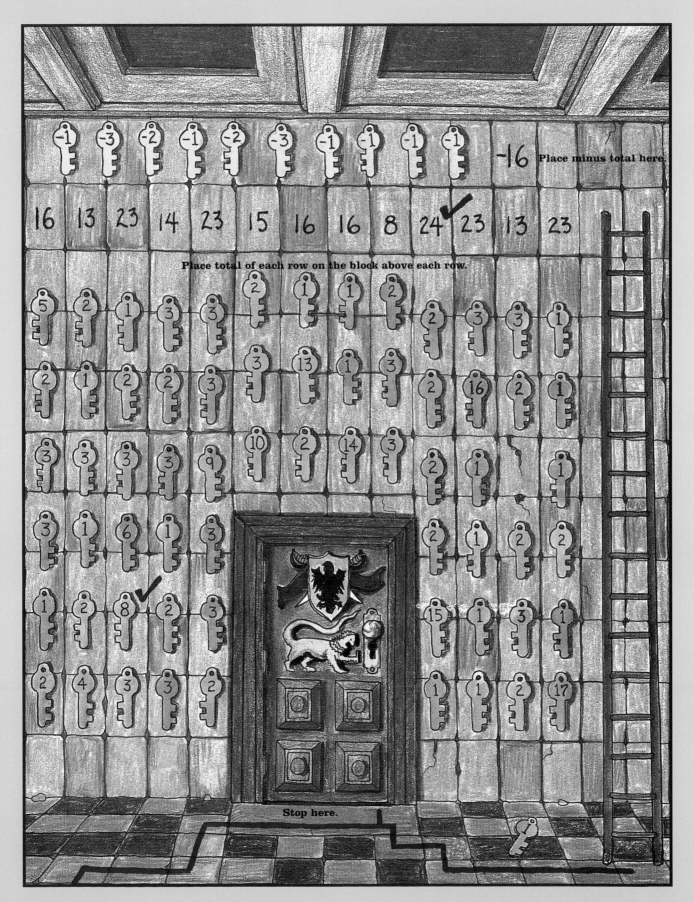

Place minus total here.

Place total of each row on the block above each row.

Stop here.

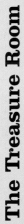

Cannon Defenses

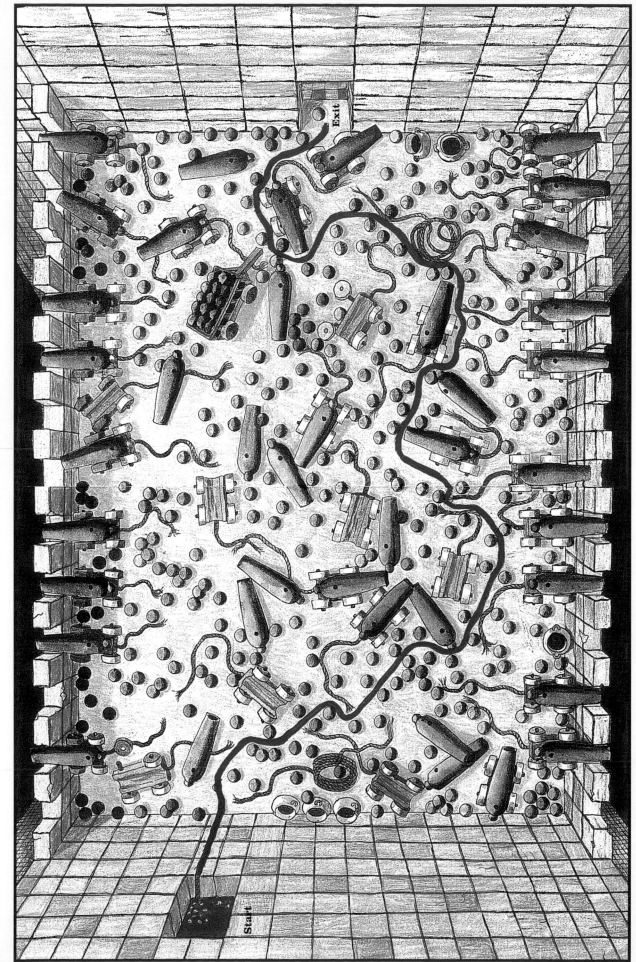

The Golden Idol

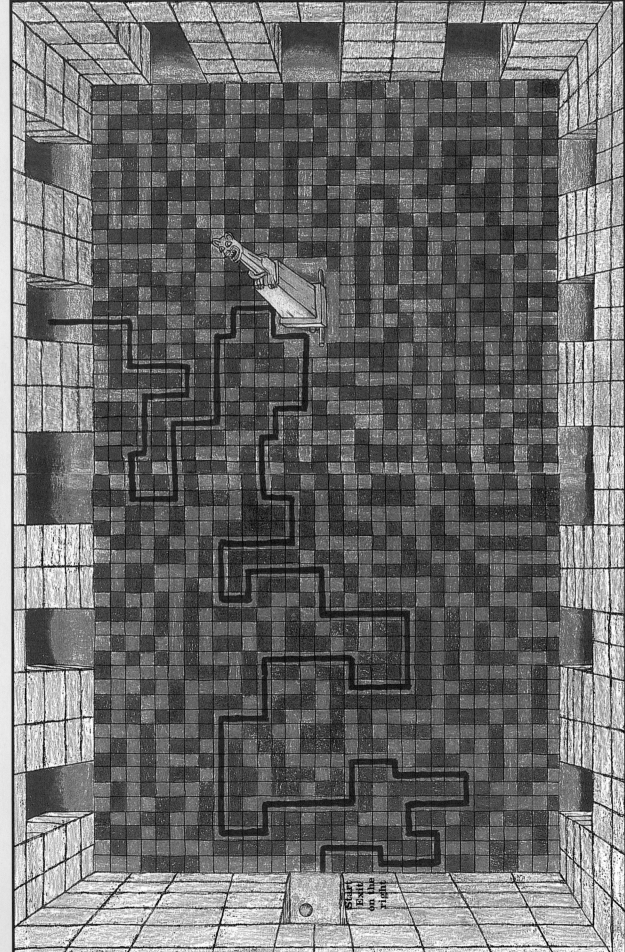

Start
Exit
on the
right